50 Delicious Taco Recipes for Every Mood

By: Kelly Johnson

Table of Contents

- Classic Beef Tacos
- Spicy Chicken Tacos
- Fish Tacos with Mango Salsa
- Veggie Tacos with Black Beans
- Pork Carnitas Tacos
- Shrimp Tacos with Avocado Cream
- Barbacoa Beef Tacos
- Grilled Vegetable Tacos
- Buffalo Cauliflower Tacos
- Breakfast Tacos with Eggs and Chorizo
- Thai Peanut Chicken Tacos
- Korean BBQ Tacos
- Baked Chicken and Cheese Tacos
- Sweet Potato and Black Bean Tacos
- Chipotle Chicken Tacos
- Carne Asada Tacos
- Greek Chicken Tacos with Tzatziki
- Lobster Tacos with Cilantro Lime Sauce
- Tofu Tacos with Spicy Peanut Sauce
- BBQ Pulled Pork Tacos
- Mediterranean Chickpea Tacos
- Pineapple Salsa Pork Tacos
- Mushroom and Spinach Tacos
- Cilantro Lime Chicken Tacos
- Jerk Chicken Tacos with Pineapple
- Fajita Steak Tacos
- Lentil Tacos with Avocado
- Sloppy Joe Tacos
- Orange-Glazed Salmon Tacos
- Roasted Beet Tacos with Goat Cheese
- Veggie and Quinoa Tacos
- Spicy Turkey Tacos
- Chicken Tinga Tacos
- Tacos al Pastor
- Bacon-Wrapped Jalapeño Popper Tacos

- Crab and Avocado Tacos
- Sriracha Honey Shrimp Tacos
- Eggplant Parmesan Tacos
- Coconut Shrimp Tacos
- Avocado and Tomato Tacos
- Banh Mi Tacos
- Cabbage and Lime Slaw Tacos
- Taco Salad in Tortilla Bowls
- Roasted Chickpea Tacos
- Chicken Fajita Tacos
- Cilantro Lime Rice and Bean Tacos
- Pesto Chicken Tacos
- Mediterranean Beef Tacos
- Sweet Chili Tofu Tacos
- Tomato and Mozzarella Caprese Tacos

Classic Beef Tacos

Ingredients:

- 1 lb ground beef
- 1 small onion, finely chopped
- 2 cloves garlic, minced
- 1 tablespoon chili powder
- 1 teaspoon ground cumin
- 1 teaspoon paprika
- ½ teaspoon salt
- ¼ teaspoon black pepper
- ¼ cup water
- 8 taco shells or tortillas
- Toppings: shredded lettuce, diced tomatoes, shredded cheese, sour cream, salsa, avocado

Instructions:

1. In a large skillet, cook the chopped onion over medium heat until it becomes translucent, about 3-4 minutes. Add the minced garlic and cook for an additional 1 minute until fragrant.
2. Add the ground beef to the skillet, breaking it up with a spatula. Cook until browned and cooked through, about 6-8 minutes. Drain excess fat if necessary.
3. Stir in the chili powder, cumin, paprika, salt, and pepper. Add the water, mixing well to combine. Simmer for 5-7 minutes until the mixture thickens slightly.
4. Warm the taco shells or tortillas according to package instructions.
5. Assemble the tacos by filling each shell with the beef mixture and adding your desired toppings. Serve immediately and enjoy!

Spicy Chicken Tacos

Ingredients:

- 1 lb boneless, skinless chicken thighs, cut into strips
- 2 tablespoons olive oil
- 1 tablespoon chili powder
- 1 teaspoon cumin
- 1 teaspoon smoked paprika
- ½ teaspoon cayenne pepper (adjust to taste)
- Salt and pepper to taste
- 8 taco shells or tortillas
- Toppings: diced onion, chopped cilantro, sliced jalapeños, avocado, sour cream, lime wedges

Instructions:

1. In a bowl, combine the chicken strips with olive oil, chili powder, cumin, smoked paprika, cayenne pepper, salt, and pepper. Mix until the chicken is well coated.
2. Heat a skillet over medium-high heat. Add the chicken and cook for 6-8 minutes until cooked through and slightly charred, stirring occasionally.
3. Warm the taco shells or tortillas according to package instructions.
4. Assemble the tacos by filling each shell with the spicy chicken and adding your desired toppings. Serve with lime wedges on the side.

Fish Tacos with Mango Salsa

Ingredients:

- 1 lb white fish fillets (like cod or tilapia)
- 1 tablespoon olive oil
- 1 teaspoon chili powder
- ½ teaspoon cumin
- Salt and pepper to taste
- 8 taco shells or tortillas
- **For Mango Salsa:**
    - 1 ripe mango, diced
    - 1 small red onion, finely chopped
    - 1 jalapeño, minced
    - Juice of 1 lime
    - Salt to taste
    - Fresh cilantro, chopped

Instructions:

1. Preheat the grill or a skillet over medium heat. Season the fish fillets with olive oil, chili powder, cumin, salt, and pepper.
2. Grill or cook the fish for about 3-4 minutes on each side, or until cooked through and flaky. Remove from heat and break into pieces.
3. For the mango salsa, combine the diced mango, red onion, jalapeño, lime juice, salt, and cilantro in a bowl. Mix gently.
4. Warm the taco shells or tortillas according to package instructions.
5. Assemble the tacos by filling each shell with the fish and topping with mango salsa. Serve immediately.

Veggie Tacos with Black Beans

Ingredients:

- 1 can (15 oz) black beans, drained and rinsed
- 1 tablespoon olive oil
- 1 red bell pepper, diced
- 1 zucchini, diced
- 1 small onion, diced
- 2 cloves garlic, minced
- 1 teaspoon cumin
- 1 teaspoon smoked paprika
- Salt and pepper to taste
- 8 taco shells or tortillas
- Toppings: shredded lettuce, diced tomatoes, avocado, salsa, lime wedges

Instructions:

1. In a skillet, heat olive oil over medium heat. Add the diced onion and garlic, and sauté until the onion is translucent, about 3-4 minutes.
2. Add the red bell pepper and zucchini, and cook for another 5 minutes until softened.
3. Stir in the black beans, cumin, smoked paprika, salt, and pepper. Cook for an additional 3-4 minutes, stirring occasionally, until heated through.
4. Warm the taco shells or tortillas according to package instructions.
5. Assemble the tacos by filling each shell with the veggie and bean mixture, then add your desired toppings. Serve with lime wedges on the side.

Pork Carnitas Tacos

Ingredients:

- 2 lbs pork shoulder, cut into chunks
- 1 onion, quartered
- 4 cloves garlic, minced
- 1 tablespoon ground cumin
- 1 tablespoon chili powder
- 1 teaspoon oregano
- 1 cup orange juice
- Salt and pepper to taste
- 8 taco shells or tortillas
- Toppings: diced onion, chopped cilantro, lime wedges, salsa

Instructions:

1. In a slow cooker, combine pork, onion, garlic, cumin, chili powder, oregano, orange juice, salt, and pepper.
2. Cook on low for 8 hours or until the pork is tender and easily shreds.
3. Shred the pork with two forks and mix with the cooking juices.
4. Warm the taco shells or tortillas according to package instructions.
5. Assemble the tacos by filling each shell with carnitas and adding your desired toppings. Serve with lime wedges on the side.

Shrimp Tacos with Avocado Cream

Ingredients:

- 1 lb shrimp, peeled and deveined
- 1 tablespoon olive oil
- 1 teaspoon chili powder
- 1 teaspoon cumin
- Salt and pepper to taste
- 8 taco shells or tortillas
- **For Avocado Cream:**
    - 1 ripe avocado
    - ½ cup sour cream
    - Juice of 1 lime
    - Salt to taste
- Toppings: shredded cabbage, chopped cilantro, lime wedges

Instructions:

1. In a bowl, toss shrimp with olive oil, chili powder, cumin, salt, and pepper.
2. Heat a skillet over medium-high heat and cook the shrimp for 2-3 minutes on each side until pink and opaque.
3. For the avocado cream, blend avocado, sour cream, lime juice, and salt until smooth.
4. Warm the taco shells or tortillas according to package instructions.
5. Assemble the tacos by filling each shell with shrimp, drizzling with avocado cream, and adding your desired toppings. Serve with lime wedges on the side.

Barbacoa Beef Tacos

Ingredients:

- 2 lbs beef chuck roast
- 1 onion, quartered
- 4 cloves garlic, minced
- 1 tablespoon ground cumin
- 1 tablespoon chili powder
- 1 teaspoon oregano
- 1 tablespoon apple cider vinegar
- 1 cup beef broth
- Salt and pepper to taste
- 8 taco shells or tortillas
- Toppings: diced onion, chopped cilantro, salsa, lime wedges

Instructions:

1. In a slow cooker, combine beef, onion, garlic, cumin, chili powder, oregano, apple cider vinegar, beef broth, salt, and pepper.
2. Cook on low for 8 hours or until the beef is tender and easily shreds.
3. Shred the beef with two forks and mix with the cooking juices.
4. Warm the taco shells or tortillas according to package instructions.
5. Assemble the tacos by filling each shell with barbacoa beef and adding your desired toppings. Serve with lime wedges on the side.

Grilled Vegetable Tacos

Ingredients:

- 1 zucchini, sliced
- 1 bell pepper, sliced
- 1 red onion, sliced
- 1 cup corn (fresh or frozen)
- 2 tablespoons olive oil
- 1 teaspoon chili powder
- Salt and pepper to taste
- 8 taco shells or tortillas
- Toppings: avocado, cilantro, lime wedges, crumbled feta (optional)

Instructions:

1. Preheat the grill to medium-high heat. In a bowl, toss the vegetables with olive oil, chili powder, salt, and pepper.
2. Grill the vegetables for about 5-7 minutes until tender and slightly charred, turning occasionally.
3. Warm the taco shells or tortillas according to package instructions.
4. Assemble the tacos by filling each shell with grilled vegetables and adding your desired toppings. Serve with lime wedges on the side.

Buffalo Cauliflower Tacos

Ingredients:

- 1 head cauliflower, cut into florets
- ½ cup buffalo sauce
- 1 tablespoon olive oil
- 8 taco shells or tortillas
- Toppings: shredded lettuce, diced tomatoes, blue cheese dressing, cilantro

Instructions:

1. Preheat the oven to 425°F (220°C). In a bowl, toss cauliflower florets with olive oil and buffalo sauce until well coated.
2. Spread the cauliflower on a baking sheet and roast for 20-25 minutes until crispy.
3. Warm the taco shells or tortillas according to package instructions.
4. Assemble the tacos by filling each shell with buffalo cauliflower and adding your desired toppings.

Breakfast Tacos with Eggs and Chorizo

Ingredients:

- 4 large eggs
- 1 cup chorizo, cooked and crumbled
- 8 taco shells or tortillas
- Toppings: diced tomatoes, avocado, shredded cheese, salsa

Instructions:

1. In a skillet, scramble the eggs over medium heat until just set.
2. Add the cooked chorizo to the skillet and stir to combine.
3. Warm the taco shells or tortillas according to package instructions.
4. Assemble the tacos by filling each shell with the egg and chorizo mixture, then adding your desired toppings.

Thai Peanut Chicken Tacos

Ingredients:

- 1 lb boneless, skinless chicken thighs, cut into strips
- 1 tablespoon olive oil
- ½ cup Thai peanut sauce
- 8 taco shells or tortillas
- Toppings: shredded carrots, cucumber slices, cilantro, lime wedges

Instructions:

1. In a skillet, heat olive oil over medium-high heat. Add chicken strips and cook until no longer pink, about 5-7 minutes.
2. Stir in the Thai peanut sauce and cook for another 2-3 minutes until heated through.
3. Warm the taco shells or tortillas according to package instructions.
4. Assemble the tacos by filling each shell with the chicken mixture and adding your desired toppings. Serve with lime wedges on the side.

Korean BBQ Tacos

Ingredients:

- 1 lb beef flank steak, sliced thin
- ¼ cup soy sauce
- 2 tablespoons brown sugar
- 1 tablespoon sesame oil
- 1 teaspoon ginger, minced
- 1 teaspoon garlic, minced
- 8 taco shells or tortillas
- Toppings: sliced green onions, shredded carrots, sesame seeds, cilantro

Instructions:

1. In a bowl, combine soy sauce, brown sugar, sesame oil, ginger, and garlic. Marinate the beef in the mixture for at least 30 minutes.
2. Heat a skillet over medium-high heat and cook the beef for 3-5 minutes until browned.
3. Warm the taco shells or tortillas according to package instructions.
4. Assemble the tacos by filling each shell with the beef and adding your desired toppings.

Baked Chicken and Cheese Tacos

Ingredients:

- 2 cups cooked chicken, shredded
- 1 cup shredded cheese (cheddar or Monterey Jack)
- 1 packet taco seasoning
- 8 taco shells
- 1 cup salsa
- Toppings: diced tomatoes, shredded lettuce, sour cream, avocado

Instructions:

1. Preheat the oven to 350°F (175°C).
2. In a bowl, mix shredded chicken with taco seasoning and half of the cheese.
3. Fill each taco shell with the chicken mixture and place them in a baking dish.
4. Pour salsa over the tacos and sprinkle the remaining cheese on top.
5. Bake for 15-20 minutes until the cheese is melted and bubbly.
6. Serve with your desired toppings.

Sweet Potato and Black Bean Tacos

Ingredients:

- 2 medium sweet potatoes, peeled and diced
- 1 can black beans, drained and rinsed
- 1 tablespoon olive oil
- 1 teaspoon cumin
- 1 teaspoon chili powder
- 8 taco shells or tortillas
- Toppings: avocado, lime wedges, cilantro, diced red onion

Instructions:

1. Preheat the oven to 400°F (200°C).
2. Toss diced sweet potatoes with olive oil, cumin, chili powder, salt, and pepper. Spread on a baking sheet and roast for 25-30 minutes until tender.
3. In a bowl, mix the roasted sweet potatoes with black beans.
4. Warm the taco shells or tortillas according to package instructions.
5. Assemble the tacos by filling each shell with the sweet potato and black bean mixture and adding your desired toppings.

Chipotle Chicken Tacos

Ingredients:

- 1 lb boneless, skinless chicken thighs
- 2 tablespoons chipotle sauce
- 1 tablespoon olive oil
- 1 teaspoon cumin
- 8 taco shells or tortillas
- Toppings: sliced avocado, chopped cilantro, diced onions, lime wedges

Instructions:

1. Preheat the grill or skillet over medium-high heat.
2. In a bowl, mix chicken with chipotle sauce, olive oil, cumin, salt, and pepper.
3. Grill or cook the chicken for about 6-7 minutes on each side until cooked through.
4. Let the chicken rest for a few minutes before slicing.
5. Warm the taco shells or tortillas according to package instructions.
6. Assemble the tacos by filling each shell with sliced chicken and adding your desired toppings.

Carne Asada Tacos

Ingredients:

- 1 lb flank steak
- 2 tablespoons olive oil
- 2 tablespoons lime juice
- 1 teaspoon cumin
- 1 teaspoon garlic powder
- 8 taco shells or tortillas
- Toppings: chopped onions, cilantro, salsa, lime wedges

Instructions:

1. In a bowl, marinate flank steak with olive oil, lime juice, cumin, garlic powder, salt, and pepper for at least 1 hour.
2. Preheat the grill to high heat and cook the steak for about 5-7 minutes per side for medium-rare.
3. Let the steak rest for a few minutes, then slice thinly against the grain.
4. Warm the taco shells or tortillas according to package instructions.
5. Assemble the tacos by filling each shell with sliced steak and adding your desired toppings.

Greek Chicken Tacos with Tzatziki

Ingredients:

- 1 lb boneless, skinless chicken breast, diced
- 2 tablespoons olive oil
- 1 teaspoon oregano
- 1 teaspoon garlic powder
- 8 taco shells or tortillas
- **For Tzatziki:**
    - 1 cup Greek yogurt
    - 1 cucumber, grated and drained
    - 1 clove garlic, minced
    - Juice of 1 lemon
    - Salt to taste
- Toppings: diced tomatoes, red onion, feta cheese

Instructions:

1. In a skillet, heat olive oil over medium-high heat. Add diced chicken, oregano, garlic powder, salt, and pepper, cooking until the chicken is cooked through.
2. For the tzatziki, mix Greek yogurt, cucumber, garlic, lemon juice, and salt in a bowl.
3. Warm the taco shells or tortillas according to package instructions.
4. Assemble the tacos by filling each shell with chicken, tzatziki, and your desired toppings.

Lobster Tacos with Cilantro Lime Sauce

Ingredients:

- 1 lb cooked lobster meat, chopped
- 1 tablespoon butter
- 1 teaspoon garlic, minced
- 8 taco shells or tortillas
- **For Cilantro Lime Sauce:**
    - ½ cup sour cream
    - ¼ cup mayonnaise
    - Juice of 1 lime
    - ¼ cup fresh cilantro, chopped
    - Salt to taste
- Toppings: shredded cabbage, diced avocado

Instructions:

1. In a skillet, melt butter over medium heat and sauté garlic until fragrant. Add lobster meat and cook for a few minutes until heated through.
2. For the cilantro lime sauce, whisk together sour cream, mayonnaise, lime juice, cilantro, and salt in a bowl.
3. Warm the taco shells or tortillas according to package instructions.
4. Assemble the tacos by filling each shell with lobster meat, drizzling with cilantro lime sauce, and adding your desired toppings.

Tofu Tacos with Spicy Peanut Sauce

Ingredients:

- 1 block firm tofu, pressed and diced
- 2 tablespoons soy sauce
- 1 tablespoon olive oil
- 1 tablespoon cornstarch
- 8 taco shells or tortillas
- **For Spicy Peanut Sauce:**
    - ¼ cup peanut butter
    - 2 tablespoons soy sauce
    - 1 tablespoon lime juice
    - 1 teaspoon sriracha (or to taste)
- Toppings: shredded carrots, chopped cilantro, lime wedges

Instructions:

1. In a bowl, toss diced tofu with soy sauce, olive oil, and cornstarch until evenly coated.
2. In a skillet, cook the tofu over medium-high heat until golden brown on all sides.
3. For the spicy peanut sauce, whisk together peanut butter, soy sauce, lime juice, and sriracha until smooth.
4. Warm the taco shells or tortillas according to package instructions.
5. Assemble the tacos by filling each shell with tofu and drizzling with spicy peanut sauce. Add your desired toppings.

BBQ Pulled Pork Tacos

Ingredients:

- 2 lbs pork shoulder
- 1 cup BBQ sauce
- 1 onion, quartered
- 8 taco shells or tortillas
- Toppings: coleslaw, pickles, sliced jalapeños

Instructions:

1. In a slow cooker, combine pork, onion, and BBQ sauce. Cook on low for 8 hours or until the pork is tender and easily shreds.
2. Shred the pork with two forks and mix with the remaining BBQ sauce.
3. Warm the taco shells or tortillas according to package instructions.
4. Assemble the tacos by filling each shell with pulled pork and adding your desired toppings.

Mediterranean Chickpea Tacos

Ingredients:

- 1 can chickpeas, drained and rinsed
- 1 tablespoon olive oil
- 1 teaspoon cumin
- 1 teaspoon smoked paprika
- 8 taco shells or tortillas
- Toppings: diced cucumber, cherry tomatoes, red onion, feta cheese, and tzatziki sauce

Instructions:

1. In a skillet, heat olive oil over medium heat. Add chickpeas, cumin, smoked paprika, salt, and pepper. Cook for about 5-7 minutes until heated through and slightly crispy.
2. Warm the taco shells or tortillas according to package instructions.
3. Assemble the tacos by filling each shell with the chickpea mixture and topping with cucumber, tomatoes, red onion, feta, and tzatziki sauce.

Pineapple Salsa Pork Tacos

Ingredients:

- 1 lb pork tenderloin
- 1 cup pineapple salsa (store-bought or homemade)
- 8 taco shells or tortillas
- Toppings: sliced avocado, cilantro, and lime wedges

Instructions:

1. Season the pork tenderloin with salt and pepper. Grill or sear until cooked through, about 15-20 minutes. Let rest before slicing.
2. Warm the taco shells or tortillas according to package instructions.
3. Assemble the tacos by filling each shell with sliced pork and topping with pineapple salsa, avocado, and cilantro.

Mushroom and Spinach Tacos

Ingredients:

- 8 oz mushrooms, sliced
- 2 cups fresh spinach
- 1 tablespoon olive oil
- 1 teaspoon garlic, minced
- 8 taco shells or tortillas
- Toppings: crumbled queso fresco, avocado, and lime wedges

Instructions:

1. In a skillet, heat olive oil over medium heat. Add mushrooms and garlic, cooking until mushrooms are browned. Stir in spinach and cook until wilted.
2. Warm the taco shells or tortillas according to package instructions.
3. Assemble the tacos by filling each shell with the mushroom and spinach mixture, then adding queso fresco and avocado.

Cilantro Lime Chicken Tacos

Ingredients:

- 1 lb boneless, skinless chicken breast, cooked and shredded
- 2 tablespoons lime juice
- 1/4 cup fresh cilantro, chopped
- 8 taco shells or tortillas
- Toppings: diced tomatoes, shredded lettuce, and sour cream

Instructions:

1. In a bowl, mix shredded chicken with lime juice, cilantro, salt, and pepper.
2. Warm the taco shells or tortillas according to package instructions.
3. Assemble the tacos by filling each shell with the chicken mixture and adding your desired toppings.

Jerk Chicken Tacos with Pineapple

Ingredients:

- 1 lb boneless, skinless chicken thighs
- 2 tablespoons jerk seasoning
- 1 cup pineapple, diced
- 8 taco shells or tortillas
- Toppings: sliced red onion, cilantro, and lime wedges

Instructions:

1. Rub chicken thighs with jerk seasoning and grill or sear until cooked through, about 6-7 minutes per side.
2. Let the chicken rest for a few minutes before slicing.
3. Warm the taco shells or tortillas according to package instructions.
4. Assemble the tacos by filling each shell with sliced jerk chicken and topping with pineapple, red onion, and cilantro.

Fajita Steak Tacos

Ingredients:

- 1 lb flank steak, sliced into strips
- 1 bell pepper, sliced
- 1 onion, sliced
- 1 tablespoon olive oil
- 8 taco shells or tortillas
- Toppings: sour cream, guacamole, and fresh cilantro

Instructions:

1. In a skillet, heat olive oil over medium-high heat. Add steak, bell pepper, and onion, cooking until the steak is browned and vegetables are tender.
2. Warm the taco shells or tortillas according to package instructions.
3. Assemble the tacos by filling each shell with the fajita mixture and adding your desired toppings.

Lentil Tacos with Avocado

Ingredients:

- 1 cup cooked lentils
- 1 tablespoon taco seasoning
- 8 taco shells or tortillas
- Toppings: diced avocado, salsa, and chopped cilantro

Instructions:

1. In a skillet, heat cooked lentils and taco seasoning over medium heat until warmed through.
2. Warm the taco shells or tortillas according to package instructions.
3. Assemble the tacos by filling each shell with the lentil mixture and adding avocado, salsa, and cilantro.

Sloppy Joe Tacos

Ingredients:

- 1 lb ground beef or turkey
- 1/2 cup ketchup
- 1 tablespoon Worcestershire sauce
- 1 teaspoon garlic powder
- 8 taco shells or tortillas
- Toppings: shredded cheese, diced onions, and pickles

Instructions:

1. In a skillet, brown the ground beef or turkey over medium heat. Drain excess fat.
2. Add ketchup, Worcestershire sauce, garlic powder, salt, and pepper, stirring to combine. Simmer for about 5 minutes.
3. Warm the taco shells or tortillas according to package instructions.
4. Assemble the tacos by filling each shell with the sloppy joe mixture and adding your desired toppings.

Orange-Glazed Salmon Tacos
Ingredients:

- 1 lb salmon fillets
- 1/4 cup orange juice
- 1 tablespoon soy sauce
- 1 tablespoon honey
- 8 taco shells or tortillas
- Toppings: sliced cabbage, cilantro, and lime wedges

Instructions:

1. Preheat the grill or oven to 400°F (200°C).
2. In a small bowl, mix orange juice, soy sauce, and honey. Brush the mixture over the salmon fillets.
3. Grill or bake the salmon for about 12-15 minutes, or until cooked through and flaky.
4. Warm the taco shells or tortillas according to package instructions.
5. Assemble the tacos by flaking the salmon into the shells and topping with cabbage, cilantro, and a squeeze of lime.

Roasted Beet Tacos with Goat Cheese

Ingredients:

- 2 medium beets, roasted and diced
- 1 tablespoon olive oil
- 8 taco shells or tortillas
- 4 oz goat cheese, crumbled
- Toppings: arugula and balsamic glaze

Instructions:

1. Preheat the oven to 400°F (200°C). Wrap beets in foil and roast for about 45-60 minutes until tender. Let cool, peel, and dice.
2. In a skillet, heat olive oil over medium heat and add diced beets, cooking for 3-5 minutes.
3. Warm the taco shells or tortillas according to package instructions.
4. Assemble the tacos by filling each shell with roasted beets, crumbled goat cheese, arugula, and drizzling with balsamic glaze.

Veggie and Quinoa Tacos
Ingredients:

- 1 cup cooked quinoa
- 1 cup mixed veggies (bell peppers, zucchini, corn)
- 1 tablespoon olive oil
- 8 taco shells or tortillas
- Toppings: avocado, salsa, and cilantro

Instructions:

1. In a skillet, heat olive oil over medium heat. Add mixed veggies and sauté until tender, about 5-7 minutes.
2. Stir in cooked quinoa and season with salt and pepper.
3. Warm the taco shells or tortillas according to package instructions.
4. Assemble the tacos by filling each shell with the veggie and quinoa mixture, topped with avocado, salsa, and cilantro.

Spicy Turkey Tacos
Ingredients:

- 1 lb ground turkey
- 1 tablespoon taco seasoning
- 8 taco shells or tortillas
- Toppings: diced tomatoes, lettuce, and jalapeños

Instructions:

1. In a skillet, cook ground turkey over medium heat until browned. Drain excess fat.
2. Stir in taco seasoning and cook for another 3-4 minutes until well combined.
3. Warm the taco shells or tortillas according to package instructions.
4. Assemble the tacos by filling each shell with the spicy turkey mixture and topping with tomatoes, lettuce, and jalapeños.

Chicken Tinga Tacos
Ingredients:

- 1 lb boneless, skinless chicken thighs, cooked and shredded
- 1 cup chipotle salsa
- 8 taco shells or tortillas
- Toppings: sliced avocado, chopped onion, and fresh cilantro

Instructions:

1. In a saucepan, combine shredded chicken and chipotle salsa. Simmer for 10 minutes to heat through.
2. Warm the taco shells or tortillas according to package instructions.
3. Assemble the tacos by filling each shell with chicken tinga and topping with avocado, onion, and cilantro.

Tacos al Pastor
Ingredients:

- 1 lb pork shoulder, thinly sliced
- 1/4 cup pineapple juice
- 2 tablespoons adobo sauce
- 8 taco shells or tortillas
- Toppings: diced pineapple, onions, and cilantro

Instructions:

1. In a bowl, marinate pork with pineapple juice and adobo sauce for at least 1 hour.
2. Grill or pan-fry the marinated pork until cooked through.
3. Warm the taco shells or tortillas according to package instructions.
4. Assemble the tacos by filling each shell with pork al pastor and topping with pineapple, onions, and cilantro.

Bacon-Wrapped Jalapeño Popper Tacos
Ingredients:

- 8 jalapeños, halved and seeded
- 8 oz cream cheese, softened
- 8 strips of bacon
- 8 taco shells or tortillas
- Toppings: shredded cheese and sour cream

Instructions:

1. Preheat the oven to 400°F (200°C).
2. Fill each jalapeño half with cream cheese and wrap with a strip of bacon. Secure with toothpicks if necessary.
3. Bake for 20-25 minutes until bacon is crispy.
4. Warm the taco shells or tortillas according to package instructions.
5. Assemble the tacos by filling each shell with bacon-wrapped jalapeños and topping with shredded cheese and sour cream.

Crab and Avocado Tacos
Ingredients:

- 1 lb lump crab meat
- 1 avocado, diced
- 1 tablespoon lime juice
- 8 taco shells or tortillas
- Toppings: cilantro and sliced radishes

Instructions:

1. In a bowl, gently mix crab meat with avocado and lime juice. Season with salt and pepper.
2. Warm the taco shells or tortillas according to package instructions.
3. Assemble the tacos by filling each shell with the crab and avocado mixture, topped with cilantro and radishes.

Sriracha Honey Shrimp Tacos
Ingredients:

- 1 lb shrimp, peeled and deveined
- 2 tablespoons sriracha
- 2 tablespoons honey
- 8 taco shells or tortillas
- Toppings: shredded cabbage, cilantro, and lime wedges

Instructions:

1. In a bowl, mix sriracha and honey. Toss the shrimp in the mixture until coated.
2. Heat a skillet over medium-high heat and cook the shrimp for 2-3 minutes on each side until pink and cooked through.
3. Warm the taco shells or tortillas according to package instructions.
4. Assemble the tacos by filling each shell with shrimp and topping with shredded cabbage, cilantro, and a squeeze of lime.

Eggplant Parmesan Tacos
Ingredients:

- 1 medium eggplant, sliced into rounds
- 1 cup marinara sauce
- 1 cup mozzarella cheese, shredded
- 8 taco shells or tortillas
- Toppings: fresh basil and grated Parmesan cheese

Instructions:

1. Preheat the oven to 375°F (190°C). Arrange eggplant slices on a baking sheet and sprinkle with salt. Let sit for 20 minutes, then pat dry.
2. Bake eggplant for 25-30 minutes until tender.
3. In a skillet, heat marinara sauce and add baked eggplant. Cook until heated through.
4. Warm the taco shells or tortillas according to package instructions.
5. Assemble the tacos by filling each shell with eggplant, topping with mozzarella, basil, and Parmesan cheese.

Coconut Shrimp Tacos

Ingredients:

- 1 lb shrimp, peeled and deveined
- 1 cup shredded coconut
- 1/2 cup breadcrumbs
- 1 egg, beaten
- 8 taco shells or tortillas
- Toppings: mango salsa and lime wedges

Instructions:

1. Preheat the oven to 400°F (200°C).
2. Dip shrimp in beaten egg, then coat with a mixture of shredded coconut and breadcrumbs.
3. Bake for 15-20 minutes until golden and crispy.
4. Warm the taco shells or tortillas according to package instructions.
5. Assemble the tacos by filling each shell with coconut shrimp and topping with mango salsa and lime.

Avocado and Tomato Tacos
Ingredients:

- 2 ripe avocados, diced
- 2 cups cherry tomatoes, halved
- 1 tablespoon lime juice
- 8 taco shells or tortillas
- Toppings: red onion and cilantro

Instructions:

1. In a bowl, combine diced avocados, cherry tomatoes, and lime juice. Season with salt and pepper.
2. Warm the taco shells or tortillas according to package instructions.
3. Assemble the tacos by filling each shell with the avocado and tomato mixture and topping with red onion and cilantro.

Banh Mi Tacos
Ingredients:

- 1 lb cooked pork (or chicken), sliced
- 1/2 cup pickled carrots and daikon
- 1 cucumber, sliced
- 8 taco shells or tortillas
- Toppings: fresh cilantro and jalapeños

Instructions:

1. Warm the cooked pork in a skillet.
2. Warm the taco shells or tortillas according to package instructions.
3. Assemble the tacos by filling each shell with pork, pickled vegetables, cucumber, and toppings of cilantro and jalapeños.

Cabbage and Lime Slaw Tacos
Ingredients:

- 4 cups shredded cabbage
- 1/4 cup lime juice
- 8 taco shells or tortillas
- Toppings: avocado and sliced radishes

Instructions:

1. In a bowl, mix shredded cabbage with lime juice and season with salt.
2. Warm the taco shells or tortillas according to package instructions.
3. Assemble the tacos by filling each shell with cabbage slaw and topping with avocado and radishes.

Taco Salad in Tortilla Bowls
Ingredients:

- 1 lb ground beef or turkey
- 1 packet taco seasoning
- 4 large tortillas
- 1 cup shredded lettuce
- 1 cup diced tomatoes
- 1 cup shredded cheese
- Toppings: sour cream and salsa

Instructions:

1. Preheat the oven to 375°F (190°C). Shape tortillas in a muffin tin to create bowls and bake for 10-15 minutes until crispy.
2. In a skillet, cook ground meat with taco seasoning according to package instructions.
3. Assemble the salad by placing meat, lettuce, tomatoes, and cheese in the tortilla bowls. Top with sour cream and salsa.

Roasted Chickpea Tacos
Ingredients:

- 1 can chickpeas, drained and rinsed
- 1 tablespoon olive oil
- 1 tablespoon taco seasoning
- 8 taco shells or tortillas
- Toppings: avocado, salsa, and cilantro

Instructions:

1. Preheat the oven to 400°F (200°C). Toss chickpeas with olive oil and taco seasoning. Spread on a baking sheet.
2. Roast for 20-25 minutes until crispy.
3. Warm the taco shells or tortillas according to package instructions.
4. Assemble the tacos by filling each shell with roasted chickpeas and topping with avocado, salsa, and cilantro.

Chicken Fajita Tacos
Ingredients:

- 1 lb chicken breast, sliced
- 1 bell pepper, sliced
- 1 onion, sliced
- 2 tablespoons fajita seasoning
- 8 taco shells or tortillas
- Toppings: sour cream, guacamole, and shredded cheese

Instructions:

1. In a skillet, heat oil over medium heat. Add chicken, bell pepper, and onion. Sprinkle fajita seasoning on top and sauté until chicken is cooked through and vegetables are tender.
2. Warm the taco shells or tortillas according to package instructions.
3. Assemble the tacos by filling each shell with the chicken and vegetable mixture. Top with sour cream, guacamole, and shredded cheese.

Cilantro Lime Rice and Bean Tacos
Ingredients:

- 1 cup cooked rice
- 1 can black beans, drained and rinsed
- 1/4 cup chopped cilantro
- Juice of 1 lime
- 8 taco shells or tortillas
- Toppings: diced avocado and salsa

Instructions:

1. In a bowl, mix cooked rice, black beans, cilantro, and lime juice. Season with salt and pepper to taste.
2. Warm the taco shells or tortillas according to package instructions.
3. Assemble the tacos by filling each shell with the rice and bean mixture. Top with diced avocado and salsa.

Pesto Chicken Tacos
Ingredients:

- 1 lb cooked chicken, shredded
- 1/4 cup pesto
- 8 taco shells or tortillas
- Toppings: arugula and cherry tomatoes

Instructions:

1. In a bowl, combine shredded chicken and pesto until well coated.
2. Warm the taco shells or tortillas according to package instructions.
3. Assemble the tacos by filling each shell with pesto chicken and topping with arugula and cherry tomatoes.

Mediterranean Beef Tacos
Ingredients:

- 1 lb ground beef
- 1 tablespoon Mediterranean seasoning (oregano, cumin, garlic powder)
- 8 taco shells or tortillas
- Toppings: cucumber, tomatoes, feta cheese, and tzatziki sauce

Instructions:

1. In a skillet, cook ground beef over medium heat. Add Mediterranean seasoning and cook until browned.
2. Warm the taco shells or tortillas according to package instructions.
3. Assemble the tacos by filling each shell with seasoned beef and topping with cucumber, tomatoes, feta cheese, and tzatziki sauce.

Sweet Chili Tofu Tacos
Ingredients:

- 1 block firm tofu, pressed and cubed
- 1/4 cup sweet chili sauce
- 8 taco shells or tortillas
- Toppings: shredded cabbage and green onions

Instructions:

1. In a skillet, heat oil over medium heat. Add cubed tofu and cook until golden brown. Pour sweet chili sauce over the tofu and stir until coated.
2. Warm the taco shells or tortillas according to package instructions.
3. Assemble the tacos by filling each shell with sweet chili tofu and topping with shredded cabbage and green onions.

Tomato and Mozzarella Caprese Tacos
Ingredients:

- 2 cups cherry tomatoes, halved
- 8 oz fresh mozzarella, diced
- 1/4 cup fresh basil, chopped
- 8 taco shells or tortillas
- Toppings: balsamic glaze

Instructions:

1. In a bowl, combine cherry tomatoes, mozzarella, and basil. Season with salt and pepper.
2. Warm the taco shells or tortillas according to package instructions.
3. Assemble the tacos by filling each shell with the tomato and mozzarella mixture. Drizzle with balsamic glaze before serving.

www.ingramcontent.com/pod-product-compliance
Lightning Source LLC
LaVergne TN
LVHW081336060526
838201LV00055B/2672